Opportunities Knock

Turning Trials into Personal Triumphs

Kevin Mangum

May the Lord
open doors of
opportunity
for you.
Kevin M

Kevin Mangum has proven himself a steady follower of Christ and a strong leader of men. His life exemplifies the kind of integrity and character for which Christian men should strive. Read this little volume, and you'll find him to have a balanced and healthy outlook on life. You'll find his sense of humor as he subtly makes fun of himself and describes the corners he's backed himself into. You'll find wisdom and depth in the truths he so ably articulates. You'll find sincerity in the practical applications that will help us apply those truths. Kevin has been youth pastor and associate pastor at my church for 11 years. I know him well, and I trust him as a true man of God.

Tim Wildmon, President
American Family Association
American Family Radio

Kevin's integrity as a teacher of the Word of God has kept me and many others coming back for more. His dry wit and sense of humor bring the principles of scripture to life. He is my pastor and dear friend and we have spent many hours laughing until our sides ached as we have enjoyed the adventure called life together.

J.J. Jasper, author, comedian, and radio host
American Family Radio

TABLE OF CONTENTS

Acknowledgements xi

Foreword.. xiii

Introduction...xvii

1. Recognizing God's Control 19

2. Allowing Circumstances to
   Strengthen Us..31

3. Knowing There are Opportunities Behind
   Problems 41

4. Learning to See Opportunities Behind
   Problems 51

5. Expecting Opportunities as Unlikely
   Candidates 63

6. **Preparing for Future Opportunities**............73

7. **Choosing Between our Plans and His Opportunities**..83

8. **Passing on a Lifestyle of Opportunity**.........91

This book is dedicated to my parents, Ken and Nancy Mangum and my mother and father-in-law, Robert and Carol Donehoo. It is also dedicated to anyone who may feel like they may have experienced more than their fair share of hard knocks in life. The Lord has tremendous opportunities waiting for you.

Acknowledgements

No man is an island, and no book is a solo project. I want to thank the following people for their contributions to this work.

Randall Murphree: For your encouragement, support, and tireless editing. This book would have never come together without you fanning the flames.

Dianne Hale and Meredith Ferris: For typing the original copy. You two are the greatest secretaries in the whole world.

Patsy West and Kimberly Walls: For editing and encouraging the work.

The Leadership and Body of First Evangelical Church: For allowing me to serve and grow in such a time as this.

Joshua, Joel, Aaron, and Anna Michelle: For bringing joy and energy into my life. I pray that the concepts in this book will rule your lives as you take advantage of God's opportunities for you.

Sherri: For your constant encouragement and support. For living the adventure with me as we watch the opportunities unfold.

The Lord Jesus Christ: For making every opportunity available through the cross.

Foreword

Kevin Mangum doesn't speak or write without having given sound and serious thought to what he has to say. Subsequently, his words always merit careful attention. Using a close call on snow skis or sinking a boat in a Honduran river as a starting point, he takes us quickly to the heart of truth – that God is offering us opportunities in every situation we encounter in life.

In the eleven years I have known him, Kevin has demonstrated that his heart is, indeed, to serve God. Because of that quality, he has earned the right to be heard. Preaching from the Sunday morning pulpit, teaching in Power House (our church's youth ministry), teaching at Global Theological Seminary in Uganda, or leading a men's study of Wild at Heart, his words are solid.

At a deeper level, I have been the beneficiary of being in a men's weekly prayer group with Kevin. In this context, I have come to know without a doubt that I can trust his motives, his heart, his insights and his commitment to Jesus Christ and to serving His people. I have also observed as he encountered various challenges and problems, some of a magnitude that would make me shudder. He prayerfully analyzes the situation, then calmly seizes the opportunity that always lies behind the problem.

His life exemplifies those key catch-phrases and qualities made popular in the men's movement of recent years—words like accountability, integrity and character. If the word daredevil were a comparable virtue, it would be there, too. You will discover in this little book that Kevin doesn't shy away from any challenge or adventure that promises an adrenaline rush.

Over the past couple of years, our church has been in a challenging transition, a part of which includes a vacant chair in the senior pastor's office. You will read Kevin's account of this unusual season in our church family, but he will not tell you how he has really stepped up to the plate. Maybe the metaphor should be that he has expertly *juggled* the plates.

It began when three full-time staffers almost simultaneously accepted calls to other avenues of ministry. So Kevin was left, abruptly and unexpectedly, to choreograph a one-man show. Now, he's quick to point out how lay leadership has also stepped up to the challenge and walked by his side all the way.

Still, the great burden lay on his shoulders. Not being in church governing leadership circles myself, but getting to pray with Kevin each week, I have been able to discern the heavy load he has sometimes felt. Through this challenge, now in its third year, Kevin and his wife Sherri have demonstrated grace, patience, wisdom, compassion, depth, maturity, perseverance and more. They will tell you it has not been easy, but they will also tell you how much they've grown in this season.

It may seem anti-climatic to follow that list of virtues with a quality stated in the negative, but David aptly defines another dimension in the character of this man. Psalm 32:2 says, "How blessed is the man to whom the Lord does not impute iniquity, and in whose spirit there is no deceit!" I have known other men who demonstrate countless Christian virtues, but who reflect deceit, anger, dismay or defeat when life throws them a curve.

Kevin and Sherri are a couple whose hearts are so set on following Jesus Christ, that they leave no room for the negatives that would hinder their growth in Him. As you read the following pages, I urge you to read with an open mind. Then live looking for an opportunity behind every challenge you face.

Randall Murphree
Editor, AFA Journal
American Family Association

Introduction

I am sure there are many other people who have thought, "I really should write a book." I have found myself saying that many times. Life has a way of putting us into many interesting situations. Those situations often demand recording. There have been enough funny, sad, or almost unbelievable things that have happened in my life that I have finally decided to write them down.

It is not that my life is that important or that I am so smart that everyone should see a glimpse of life through my eyes. Rather, I think my life's journey has been wrapped in timeless truths that can help us all get a better handle on how to face adversity in life. I think my story offers an opportunity to shine a spotlight not on me, but on some of life's principles we can all employ to help us weather the storms of life.

Some of the stories that I find myself telling about my life are so surreal that I wonder if they really happened. But they did. My precious wife, Sherri, often reminds me that with each of our lives, God is writing a story. And how we respond to the storyline determines how much glory and honor the Hero will receive.

Once again it is not that my life is so noteworthy that it should be written about. But the "Hero" and the principles are noteworthy and **must** be written about.

I am a 39-year-old associate pastor in a 500-member church in Tupelo, Mississippi. I have a beautiful wife and four awesome children. But my life journey has taken me from Tupelo to Timbuktu. I have had the rare opportunities to ride on the back of a shark, shake a leprous person's stub of a hand, travel the globe, sink a boat in a Honduran lagoon, serve as a single staff member in a 500-member church, and hold my wife's hand on a Christmas morning when a miscarriage prematurely took our second child to be with Jesus on both of their birthdays.

However, don't be fooled, the book is not about me. It is about the Hero and the Author of my story and how He guides me through this life, He has taught me in the best and worst of situations to find opportunities behind every problem. That is what this book is about. We all have eight opportunities that help us find God's opportunities behind life's problems.

Each chapter defines one of these opportunities. These opportunities help give perspective in the midst of life's trials. The opportunities are defined by Biblical principles and healthy positive thinking, and are illustrated by stories from my life and from the life of a great character from the Bible. That character is Joseph. Joseph's life is filled with life's turmoil, but he consistently takes advantage of God's opportunities. Joseph's life magnifies the principles of this book far more than mine does. There is much to learn from how he takes advantage of God's opportunities.

So, hang on for the ride. My prayer would be that some of the opportunities listed in the chapters of this book will help us to look differently at the challenging circumstances that face us. As I thought on the ideas in this book, my perspective changed about life, problems, and opportunities. It is a healthy process to see the cup as half full, instead of half empty. So read on...because **opportunities knock**.

CHAPTER 1

RECOGNIZING GOD'S CONTROL

There I was in a howling snowstorm at the top of the Outback Summit in Keystone, Colorado. The wind was blowing straight across the top of this mountain peak at ferocious speeds. Snow and ice crystals were like a thousand needles penetrating any exposed skin. The wind was so strong that even staying upright in my ski boots was a challenge.

At times visibility was less than ten feet. Fear rushed my heart and mind, and even though it was about -20 degrees Fahrenheit, I could feel the sweat from fear drenching my many layers of ski gear. All I could think was, "What am I doing here?" "What was I thinking?" and "Dear God, please, help me despite my foolishness."

And then it was like a still small voice spoke to me, "You know why you are here, Kevin. It is because of you. You are always up for a challenge and adventure. It was your feet that walked through the gate and past the sign that read "Warning! Hazardous Terrain—Avalanche Area—Expert skiers only past this point. Ski at your own risk." And of course I am not an expert skier. But what in the world did that little detail have to do with my pursuit of a thrill?

Nevertheless, I stood there frozen with cold and fear. Should I go back or walk ahead in the blinding ice and snow to see what lay ahead? Visibility was so poor that I imagined it would be easier for the edge of the peak of the mountain to find me before I found it.

Then I heard his voice, "Come on, you wanted to do this, now do it." It was Jason. All of the sane skiers in our party had headed down a nice intermediate run wagging their heads at my foolishness. They saw it coming. As soon as I saw the hazardous terrain sign, I got that strange twinkle in my eye that only comes on the heels of a testosterone and adrenaline infusion. Then I touted, "Who wants to try THAT with me?"

As the wiser in our party turned to ski away from madness, Jason and I started the ascent hiking up past the gate toward the peak. He had the skills and experience to try it; I just lacked the common sense to know any better. Would I keep hiking against the wind and chilling conditions or go back?

We kept hiking and going further away from eyeshot of civilized people. With every step the elements of cold, wind, fear, and stinging ice grew more intense. But isn't that the way it is with this adventure we call life? With each step the pressures of life become more intense. The elements of this life become unbearable and we just want to quit. And then God sends a ray of hope.

Ahead of us I could see another shadowy adventurer with a snowboard. His gear, confidence, and look of determination confirmed that he knew what he was doing and had been here before. I yelled, "What's the best way down?" Apparently the elements carried my pitiful words three peaks away, so I tried again, only louder… "What's the best way down?" This time I got his attention. He could tell by looking at me in my Sam's Wholesale Club ski gear, that what I really meant was, "What is the easiest way down?"

He called back into the wind and pointed towards the invisible edge. "The lip is pretty gnarly, dude. It is about a 10 foot straight drop. But if you work your way around the lip of the bowl to the right it lets off easier. The bowl is great! The powder is awesome! You can do it, go ahead, dude." And then his shadowy figure disappeared into blinding snow.

That was all I needed. I needed a companion and some advice from a weathered fellow traveler who had been that way before. Jason and I worked our way around the right side of the major drop off and finally identified an edge. I could tell that the lip was definitely more extreme to the left, but there was enough straight drop-off that any of it was going to be a challenge and a leap of faith for me. I worked my way to the lip, stuck my ski tips over the edge, and gulped.

Jason slid over the edge and disappeared behind the wall of snow and ice that separated us. I didn't hear him screaming for a helicopter rescue, so I dug my poles in and pushed. After surviving the lip and cutting a couple of trails, I fell into the 3-foot deep powdery snow to get my bearings. I caught my breath, and thanked God that I was still alive. As I gathered my senses, I couldn't believe my eyes.

Calm. Blue skies. Soft snow and a beautiful tree line below that resembled sanity and civilization. I couldn't believe it. I looked back towards the peak. I could see the weather, the elements, and the howling, ice-filled wind cutting across the lip of the mountain.

But the mountain itself separated the storm from the calm. In the protection of the bowl there was peace, safety, serenity, beauty, and the hope of a safe return. I looked back up at the lip and recognized a tiny figure at the most extreme point. It was the other "dude". He leapt off the snowy wall lip, aced the steepest and most extreme part of the bowl, and carved a beautiful serpentine S down the face, through the bowl, and into the tree line below.

I lay there in the snow soaking it all in. The picture captured life to me. As weary travelers, we all sometimes find ourselves assailed by the storms of life. The biting elements make the journey unbearable at times. And yet there is a mountain that separates our storms from a perfect, tranquil calm. The mountain is God. And when we tip our skis and place all our faith in His might, we enter the tranquil calm.

Even in the worst of storms, He is ever present, intimately close, and always eager to protect us from the elements and fear that often steal our will and drive to survive. He will even send us a companion, a guide, a more experienced adventurer, or a messenger from time to time to remind us that we can make it and that everything is going to be fine when we are protected by God.

I made it off the mountain that day. I am sure it wasn't pretty, or nearly as graceful as Jason or "dude", yet I long to go back. I long to go back to a beautiful, yet scary place where I learned Opportunity #1: WE HAVE THE OPPORTUNITY TO RECOGNIZE THAT GOD IS IN CONTROL.

The Storms of Life

Many of us find ourselves in a place much like the storm on top of the Outback Bowl at Keystone. The trials of life are scary, and the circumstances sting like darts. Marital failure, business failure, rebellious children, financial distress, and other difficult circumstances leave many just wishing they could get off the stormy mountain. Having worked in church ministry for nearly twenty years it has become apparent that the storms of life wreak havoc with every person and family that I have known at one time or another. Almost every week I find myself encouraging people to seek regular counseling just to handle life's trials.

Some of you reading this are in the midst of some of the most trying days of your life. One fact that you can rest assured of is that you are not alone. Difficult times are no respecter of persons. They come to all of us. For those who read this and find themselves in the midst of smooth sailing, there are probably recent days reminiscent of the destruction that the storms of life can leave behind.

The ever increasing number of people who are diagnosed with clinical depression is an indicator that more and more people wish they could escape the trials of life. Scores of people find themselves trapped in a sea of negative circumstances and see no way out. The more they focus on the storms and trials, the more bleak the situation appears to be.

Many need to see past the storms to the calm on the other side. Experience teaches that most of the time the storms of life only last for a season. Just as life brings hard times, it also brings good times. It is easier for us to appreciate the good times when we have weathered the bad. But, instead of only looking for the storm to pass, we should look for the calm that is in the middle of every storm. That calm is the fact that no matter how difficult things get, God is still in control. A mirror image to the truth that life is full of problems is the truth that God is in control.

Some people face very difficult situations. Their circumstances are so hard that they would have a difficult time believing or accepting the fact that God is in control. I have had the privilege of growing up in the United States of America. Admittedly, in this land of plenty, the storms we generally face are mild compared to the storms in other places in the world.

I have also had the privilege of spending time in the war-torn and famine-ravaged country of Uganda in East Africa. The storms are present in both countries but one would have to admit that they are more intense in Africa. Yet, in the midst of the incredible differences between these two cultures there is something refreshingly similar. There are people in both places who trust God to be their peace in the middle of their storm.

The book *Lost Boy No More* by DiAnn Mills and Abraham Nhial records the story of young men orphaned by the war in Southern Sudan. The boys are left to defend themselves against sickness, famine, war, wild animals, discouragement, defeat, and death. There are few people in the world today who could claim to have more desperate situations than these young children. But their story is an incredible story of hope and trust in a God who is in control of even the most horrible situations that life could present.

Abraham Nhial was one of those children. Now an adult living in the U.S., Abraham says, "I didn't want to starve or be killed by enemy fire. God had seen me through the dangers before, and I believed He would again. I prayed. I read my Bible. And I prayed some more."[1] Abraham had a faith in a God who was in control even in the worst of situations. No matter what storm we may face we can take comfort in the fact that God is in control.

The Stormy Life of Joseph

In Genesis chapters 30-50, the story of a young man named Joseph rises to the surface. Joseph's life is characterized by both life-altering trials and the over-arching truth that God is in control. But Joseph had a way of turning every negative problem into an opportunity for positive growth. A look at some of the highlights of his life will further drive home Opportunity #1: We have the opportunity to recognize that God is in control.

Joseph's birth sets the stage for his life. In Genesis 30:22-24 God remembers Joseph's mother, Rachel, and she conceives Joseph. Joseph is twelfth in the birth order behind ten half-brothers and one half-sister. Joseph's dad was Jacob, the father of the twelve tribes of Israel.

Jacob had six sons and one daughter by Leah, who was Joseph's aunt and stepmother. Jacob also had two sons by Joseph's mother's handmaiden, Bilhah. There were also two sons by Joseph's aunt's handmaiden, Zilpah. And finally, Joseph was born to Rachel, his father's favorite wife. The family situation that Joseph was born into was a literal breeding ground for envy and jealousy.

In Joseph's family there are four jealous matriarchal personalities. Two are sisters who are constantly trying to one up each other. The other two are handmaids who are used by Rachel and Leah to bring hurt to each other. Eleven children later, Joseph is born nearly last to the favored wife, Rachel. This makes him the favorite son.

Now he is not only the runt, but also his eleven siblings are jealous of him. To make it worse, after he is born, his mother proclaims: "May the Lord give me another son" (Genesis 30:24). Even upon his long awaited arrival, Joseph was not enough to please his mother. Joseph's family was full of jealousy and fighting. He was picked on by older siblings, and was not enough to please or satisfy a jealous, discontent mom. You just thought you had family problems.

Promise Behind the Problems

Regardless of Joseph's predicament in the family order, God's sovereignty held hope. Since God is in control, Joseph's situation also had an up side. Even at his birth, there is a glimpse of hope and God's promise. When Rachel bears Joseph, she not only requests the birth of another son, she also states, "God had taken away my reproach" (Genesis 30:23). That reproach was Rachel's barrenness.

While Joseph's birth was a relief to Rachel's childlessness, this was not the only disgrace that is lifted through the birth of Joseph. Joseph's life not only represented the end of barrenness, but also would eventually represent the end of the reproach of famine, starvation, and the ultimate destruction of his entire family tree. Joseph's life purpose of rescuing the family from despair overshadows the problems he faces in his family. The fact that God is in control always overshadows the fact that life brings many problems.

This truth is exemplified in any life which is lived for God's purposes.

Joseph had an unusual sense that his life was more than what his family tree would limit him to. His story picks up again in Genesis 37, where he had two dreams. The two dreams revealed that Joseph would eventually have rule and dominion over not only his older brothers, but also his mother and father. When Joseph decided to share these dreams with the family, his news was not well received. Three times the passage emphasizes that his brothers hated him even more for the dreams (Genesis 37:4, 5, and 8).

Despite the hatred, Joseph believed the dreams. Surely it was hard at times to believe what had been shown to him in the dreams. But the story line seems to show that Joseph was more focused on the dream and the Dream Giver than on the circumstances of life. Joseph chose to seize Opportunity #1. No matter how difficult life is—recognize that God is in control. Joseph understood God's sovereignty.

God's Sovereignty

A belief in God's sovereignty is made up of several components. If you believe that God is sovereign, it means that you believe God rules over everything. The belief starts by saying that God is in control, but it even goes beyond that.

When you can't see His hand,
you can trust His heart.

God's sovereignty indicates that His purposes prevail even when the circumstances show otherwise. God's all-powerful reign is the driving force behind a saying like,

"When you can't see His hand, you can trust His heart." He is in control. He is superior to the circumstances and His purposes will be accomplished.

In Isaiah 28:21, Scripture says, "For the LORD will rise up...that He may do His work, His awesome work, and bring to pass His act, His unusual act" (New King James Version*)*.

In this verse it is apparent that the sovereign God will make Himself known. It also clarifies that He has a work to do. This is a work that He will bring to pass. He will complete it in His time. The verse also states that His work is an unusual act. This is a reminder that His thoughts are not our thoughts and His ways are not our ways

Isaiah 55:9 goes on to say, "For as the heavens are higher than the earth, so are My ways higher than your ways, and My thoughts than your thoughts." God wants us to see that even when things do not seem to make sense, He is in control and His plan is bigger than ours.

He is able and He waits for his followers to see Him as in control. Many times the circumstances are allowed to continue to bring an unyielding trust in His control.

In the storm at the top of the mountain, God's control, God's peace, and God's calm were just a leap of faith away from being reality. Prior to the leap, all that could be realized were stormy conditions. The reality of Joseph's dream was based on his knowledge that God is in control. No matter where we find ourselves, we have the opportunity to see the same reality, God is in control.

---

[1] DiAnn Mills and Abraham Nhial, *Lost Boy No More* (Nashville, Broadman and Holman, 2004).

Opportunities for Discussion

1. Have you ever found yourself in a situation where you had to completely rely on God's control?

   Yes _____ No _____

   If yes, briefly describe it below.

   _____

   _____

   _____

2. What storms of life make it hard for you to believe God is in control?

   _____

   _____

   _____

   _____

3. How did Joseph see beyond his circumstances to trust in the dream that God had given him?

   _____

   _____

   _____

4. In what circumstances do you need to apply Opportunity #1 in your life right now?

_____

_____

_____

_____

CHAPTER 2

ALLOWING CIRCUMSTANCES TO STENGTHEN US

There I was with tears running down my face, staring at the freshly broken ground. The previous weeks had held a series of events so staggering that movies and books should be made to tell the story. The ground I was staring at in stunned silence was the ground that lies in front of the 500-member church where I serve as associate pastor. The church had four full-time pastoral staff positions: pastor, worship pastor, youth pastor, and children's pastor. A new small groups pastor was to be added later that same year.

The pastor and worship leader had served together for close to fifteen years, and I had served with them for nine years. Having come from a previous church staff in which there was conflict, these present staff relationships had been a dream come true for me. We were not only peers in ministry, but the best of friends. We were the church staff. However, now all that had changed.

On one Sunday, the children's minister of three years resigned to stay at home with her new baby. The next Sunday the church broke ground for a four million dollar building project to be done without debt and only about half of that amount had been raised. The following month changed everything and would change me forever.

My two colleagues were both called by God to serve together at another church and they resigned within the month after the ground breaking. Man could not plan such timing. Many men and women would question God's planning such timing. Our church and my career were proceeding along comfortably just as we planned. However, sometimes the God of all creation sees fit to shake the comfortable surroundings in which we find ourselves. But if Opportunity #1 is true—and it is—God was in control of this whole new set of seemingly negative circumstances.

As I stared out the window at the dozer and the freshly moved dirt, I felt alone, confused, and inadequate. At this critical time, I wondered if I was up to leading the body of believers who would one day worship on that freshly turned spot. Would it be the end of me? I knew that I was about to be stretched, but I wondered if I would be shattered.

Questions raced through my dazed mind. Why would God do this to me? Why would God trust me to leave me as the single staff member in such circumstances? Had I done something wrong or maybe something right? How lonely would I be on this journey? Will I survive this test? And finally, the more human thought...*I wonder if they need a youth pastor where my friends are going?*

I only know one thing. I was resolved to do whatever God wanted me to, because He is in control. He knows best even when it doesn't seem that anything good could come out of a situation.

The next week an opportunity to escape knocked at my door. A pastor friend called and asked if I would be interested in pastoring a church in the Caribbean. He knew that I had a heart for missions work and he knew of a church in Barbados that needed a pastor. My initial thought was: *Steeple plus sand and ocean plus a hammock must equal*

God's will. I could have punched myself in the eye as I heard the words come out of my mouth: "No, I need to see the church through this time." What was I thinking?

The answer to that question still evades me. But I think I know what my sovereign God was thinking. I *wanted* an opportunity to escape. But I *needed* an opportunity to grow. That brings us to Opportunity #2: WE HAVE THE OPPORTUNITY TO ALLOW ANY CIRCUMSTANCE TO STRENGTHEN US. I did not know it then, but these circumstances were my opportunity to grow and be stretched like never before.

"Don't Pray for Patience"

Have you ever heard it said, "Don't pray for patience" or "Don't pray for faith"? People who say that probably have an understanding that patience, faith, and growth are usually produced by experiencing trials. James 1:2-4 outlines the process well:

> Consider it all joy, my brothers, when you encounter various trials, knowing that the testing of your faith produces endurance, and let endurance have its perfect result, so that you may be perfect and complete, lacking nothing.

The very thought of this verse is a bit humorous. How many of us get really happy about hard times coming our way? Not many. Most of us would rather skip the trials and the growth for the sake of smooth sailing. Only those with a real understanding of what it takes to grow can appreciate these verses. These people also understand Opportunity #2: We have the opportunity to allow any circumstance to strengthen us.

Signs of Testing and Strength

I recently was given a gift certificate for an hour of Swedish massage. I was about 45 minutes into my "out of body experience" when the therapist began to work on my left calf. His technique changed and he seemed to be working harder on that muscle. Soon he said, "You must really work this leg hard." I had him fooled. He thought Mr. Universe had let me borrow his left calf.

However, the principle behind Opportunity #2 was in place. I told him that muscle's history. I had torn the left calf in half in a skiing accident about ten years earlier. To compensate, the muscle had to strengthen itself. What was left of it was apparently the toughest, grainiest muscle in my whole body. It got that way through extreme trial.

The same principle is at work in the life of a dear saint of God in my church. Norma had wrestled with cancer for several years. She had endured extreme medications, energy loss, hair loss, invasive surgery, and many of the other endurance-building trials that come with cancer. During the course of this trial, Norma's walk with Jesus became sweeter and sweeter.

The greater the trial is,
the greater the growth can be.

After a period of time her cancer went into remission and she was given a clean bill of health by her doctors. One day when I was talking with her about her experience she said, "I would not trade any of what I went through with the cancer, because of what I gained in my relationship with Christ. My Savior has been so sweet to me in all this." Norma understood that any experience can bring an opportunity for us to grow stronger.

Norma's story reflects a principle that is often in place in our lives. That principle is, the greater the trial is, the greater the growth can be.

Joseph's Chance to Grow

Joseph also learned that trials bring growth. In Genesis 37:18 Joseph's brothers had become fed up with his dreaming big dreams. They devised a plan to kill him. They threw him into a waterless pit with the intention of leaving him to die. After thinking about it, the brothers saw a different type of opportunity knocking.

Judah said to his brothers, "What profit is it for us to kill our brother and cover his blood? Come let us sell him as a slave...for he is our own flesh." What a great brother! Instead of killing him, they could just sell him. This plan would be easier, less messy, less of a burden of guilt, and besides, they would make some money!

God used this trial as a beginning point for Joseph. It was his first real test of strengthening. The rejection by his brothers was Joseph's first step towards success. And his success would come back around to save his brothers. Later in Joseph's life, he sees his brothers again and has an opportunity to either seek revenge or spare their lives.

His words are a great example of understanding that our difficult circumstances can be used to strengthen us. Joseph understood that any circumstance, even rejection by family, could be used to strengthen him. He says:

"Do not be afraid, for am I in God's place? (Opportunity #1: God is in control). As for you, you meant evil against me, but God meant it for good in order to bring about this present result, to preserve many people alive. So, therefore, do not be afraid;

I will provide for you and your little ones. So he comforted them and spoke kindly to them" (Genesis 50:19-21).

Joseph had allowed the pain that his brothers inflicted upon him to strengthen him. Joseph understood that behind his negative situation there was an opportunity to grow. He had a good understanding of Opportunity #2 and the strengthening power of life's troubles.

The Source of Problems

Opportunity #2 doesn't often make much sense. It is not natural to get excited about bad things happening. We don't often welcome trouble and trials. And beyond that, trials typically shake our faith and trust in God's control. When bad things happen, the most natural response is to question why those events happened. That is the human response. Recognizing opportunities behind life's problems is not a typical or natural response. Recognizing opportunities is a response that comes from a foundation of knowing that God is in control.

Since God's control is often questioned in the face of trials, it is important to identify where trials and problems come from.

While it is not in the scope of this book to give a theological explanation for the problem of evil and why bad things happen, it must be addressed to affirm that God is in control. First, it must be established that God is all powerful and in control. Secondly, it must be clarified that He allows men to choose to obey Him or listen to their own appetite to do wrong.

All the way back to the Garden of Eden, man has not chosen to follow God's prescribed plan for our lives. Many of life's problems and trials can be linked to consequences of our own disobedience. The closer we live to God's prescribed plan for our lives, the less we will face negative circumstances. However, the curse of the fall has set in motion consequences on both man's selfish nature and the earth itself. As a result, all of us are affected by negative circumstances.

It is important to recognize that while God has ultimate authority over all of these circumstances, He is not the source of evil, problems and trials. Our own tendency towards disobedience is the source of most evil, problems, and trials. This explains how it can be stated that even though there are problems and trials present, God is good and He is in control.

Most of life's storms can be traced back to either nature or natural consequences. Nature itself was changed by man's choice to obey desires instead of deity. In Genesis 3:17 God says to Adam and Eve, "Cursed is the ground because of you; in the toil you shall eat of it all the days of your life. Both thorns and thistles it shall grow for you." The fall led to thorns and thistles. Prior to the fall, the earth was a perfect environment. After the fall, nature had problematic features.

Thorns and thistles are the light end of things. It is the tornadoes and tidal waves that make men question God's level of control. God is not the source of these natural problems, but He is their authority. He has allowed the course of the curse to play out. It is His mercy that keeps these natural disasters from being worse. During the writing of this book, the worst natural disaster in many years has taken place. The tsunami in the Indian Ocean claimed the lives of over 288,000 people. While God was not the source of this event, He did allow the fault lines in the Indian Ocean to take their natural course. It is His mercy that spared many and allowed incredible opportunities for the survivors. Many disastrous trials are a direct result of nature.

Other trials come as a result of natural consequences. These trials or problems are natural consequences that come out of our poor decision making. God allows us to face the consequences of our poor choices.

I recently lost a loved one to a heart attack. Some ask, "Why would God allow such a thing to happen?" The diagnosis of the doctor made the answer pretty plain. The doctor said that after 45 years of smoking, such a heart attack could be expected. While the loss of life was tragic, it was not without explanation. The explanation couldn't be blamed on a God who is in control.

No matter the source of our trials, God shows us favor by allowing certain trials to strengthen us and our trust in Him. He does not make bad things happen to His children. It is important to see man's sin as the source of evil and problems. God allows these things to happen, but walks beside us to help us recognize the opportunity behind the problems.

The temptation for us when trials come is to blame God or be angry at Him. As established by these first two opportunities, God is in control and He does want to strengthen us. If these two things are true—and they are— then our best response to trials is to acknowledge His control over and love for our lives and then identify the ways that He may want to grow us through uncomfortable circumstances. While this is not the easiest or the most natural response to difficulty, it is the best way to face trials. We should look for God's opportunities where they may be hiding.

The purpose of this book is to move us beyond identifying why bad things happen. It is the heart of this work to help us move past the difficulties to see the opportunities. Many times we spend a great deal of time trying to establish why something happened. Most of the time that process is difficult. God is far more concerned with our response to life's problems than that we figure out why they happened. The biggest question is "What will we make of the situation in which we find ourselves?"

Opportunities for Discussion

1. What was the time of greatest personal growth in your life?

   _____

   _____

   _____

2. Were there trials related to the events listed in question 1? If so list them.

   _____

   _____

   _____

3. Read James 1:2-4. How have these verses been a reality in your life?

   _____

   _____

   _____

4. Read Genesis 37:18ff. How would you have reacted if you were Joseph?

_____

_____

_____

5. What trials are in your life now that may be an opportunity to strengthen you?

_____

_____

CHAPTER 3

KNOWING THERE ARE OPPORTUNITIES BEHIND EVERY PROBLEM

There I was covered in blood and helpless. I did not know what to do, nor did I personally have the resources to take care of myself. I was injured and weak and could not even tend to my own needs. I couldn't feed myself, heal my wounds, or get away from the mess I was in. I was truly in the biggest problem of my life.

To tell you the truth, that incident, my birth, was a real problem. I was born at home in my parents' room without a doctor's care. To that time in my life, no one had taught me the etiquette principle which suggests you should not show up at someone's house abruptly and without adequate advanced warning. From the beginning of my life, my very existence has had the potential to be a major problem...or an opportunity.

My birth could have been the event that brought my parents together or the wedge that would drive them apart. My existence presented the chance to raise a son who could one day make a difference in his world or it presented a chance for bitterness. Ten years later, time would reveal that while my parents chose to care for and raise a son, their marriage could not withstand the problems that weighed against it. And again I became a problem.

Every child of divorce presents problems. Children in a divorce are the only real permanent things that require the divided parents to communicate. In too many cases, the children become a bargaining chip or a place for parents to vent all of their frustrations from the failure of the relationship. As a result, my parents' divorce when I was ten years old is the most difficult thing I have ever had to endure.

God however, used my biggest problem to lead to my biggest asset. Soon after my parents' divorce, I went for counseling with our church's pastor. In that meeting I invited Christ into my life and He became my Savior. The pastor showed me that I could trust God even with the pain of my parents' divorce. It didn't stop there. God continued to make lemonade out of lemons. The trials that came from the breakup were used by God to shape who I am.

Throughout the next ten years of my life, the separation made me independent and determined, and eventually made me very dependent on Christ's strength. Through this trial, Christ also gave me a hunger and determination to have a marriage one day that could withstand the storms of life. With God in control, the biggest problem in my life became my greatest opportunity.

Proactive or Reactive

Someone has said, "Behind every problem there is an opportunity." This is the basis of Opportunity #3: WE HAVE THE OPPORTUNITY TO KNOW THERE ARE OPPORTUNITIES BEHIND EVERY PROBLEM. It has already been established that life itself presents many problems. Imagine the potential there is in life if there is an opportunity behind every problem.

This is not to say that we should go out looking for problems. But when problems come, we should look hard to see if there is an opportunity behind the problem. Most of the time our reaction to the problem determines whether or not we will see the opportunity.

In Stephen Covey's book *The Seven Habits of Highly Effective People*, the first habit is that a person should think proactively.[1] This means that we are responsible for our own lives and are responsible for how we respond to life. A proactive person takes initiative to positively affect his surroundings. Reactive people have little initiative and find themselves controlled by and affected by their problems or surroundings. In short, we can either act or be acted upon, and it is our choice.

Recently an elder in my church had a terrible accident. Dr. Max Hutchinson is a cardiologist who loves to hunt. On a cool fall morning, he had headed off to hunt by himself. Early that morning he fell some 25 feet from his tree stand. The impact of the fall broke a rib, burst a portion of his small intestine, caused a hairline fracture in one elbow, and shattered several bones in his other wrist and forearm. In a sheer act of adrenaline, he drove himself to get help. He was air lifted back to the hospital where he operates, but this time he was to be the patient. Over the next several days, the Lord and other capable doctors repaired his injuries.

As one might expect, a three-month recovery period and the inability to use the badly injured arm were not good news for a skilled surgeon. His arms and hands are his most valuable tools, but they had sustained the worst of the injuries. He could have seen this as a time to be discouraged and to give up, but instead he saw an opportunity to be proactive behind the problem.

Over the next three months, Dr. Max seized the opportunity to be proactive with the time he had on his hands. He invested himself in extra study time, in building and strengthening his marriage, and in serving his church. Instead of complaining about missed work time and the pain of recovery, he allowed God to show him the opportunities behind the accident. He was also careful to give God the praise for sparing his life instead of complaining about the injuries. In one conversation he shared with me how glad he was that he got to spend time investing in his own life, marriage, and church during a difficult, but special time for him.

That is what being proactive is about. It takes a positive, proactive attitude to let God show us how to take difficult times and turn them into productive times. It is the type of attitude that sees the cup as half full instead of half empty.

Joseph as the Cupbearer

Joseph was definitely one who saw the cup as half full instead of half empty. Joseph was sold into slavery by his brothers and was eventually purchased to be the personal servant, the "cupbearer" if you will, to Potiphar, the captain of Pharaoh's bodyguard in Egypt. In Genesis 39:1-6, Joseph was put in charge of everything that Potiphar owned:

> Now Joseph had been taken down to Egypt; and Potiphar, an Egyptian officer of Pharaoh, the captain of the bodyguard, bought him from the Ishmaelites, who had taken him down there. *And the Lord was with Joseph,* so he became a successful man. And he was in the house of his master, the Egyptian. Now his master saw that the Lord was with him and how *the Lord caused all that he did to prosper in his hand.* So Joseph found favor in his sight, and became his personal servant; and he made him overseer over his house, and all that he owned he put in his charge. And it came about that from that time he made him overseer in his house, and over all that he owned, *the Lord blessed the Egyptian's house on account of*

Joseph; thus the Lord's blessing was upon all that he owned, in the house and in the field. So he left everything he owned in Joseph's charge; and with him there he did not concern himself with anything except the food which he ate. Now Joseph was handsome in form and appearance. (Emphases added)

Three times in these four verses Scripture states that Joseph became successful and that the Lord caused everything he touched to prosper. It even states that Potiphar's entire house was blessed because of Joseph.

Joseph was proactive. He realized that behind his greatest problems, there were opportunities. Joseph did not dwell on his problems or his slavery. He continued to trust God despite the obvious circumstances. Though rejected by family and sold as a slave, Joseph soon became the most successful and desired servant in Egypt. He did not become prosperous by lying around cursing his family and complaining about his work load.

He trusted God and made the most of his situation, even his problems. He knew that God was in control. He knew that his problems could be used to strengthen him. And he experienced opportunity #3 as he saw that some of his greatest opportunities in life could be found right behind some of its greatest challenges. Joseph seized those opportunities and was blessed by God for it.

Real Life

As I write about opportunities behind every problem, gnawing questions may continue to arise: "You don't know my problems; there can't be any opportunities behind a problem this big, can there?" or "Don't you know the problems in the world: starvation, war, disease, and death; can there really be an opportunity behind some of these major unexplainable problems?" These are legitimate questions that test the very thoughts of this book. Two points seem to address these questions.

First, the illustrations that are used in this book include the most difficult ones that can be faced in life. In most of the illustrations someone has made the most of opportunities behind these difficult problems. Cancer, divorce, job difficulties, family rejection, famine, natural disasters, and slavery have already been addressed. Joseph's life in itself illustrates some of the biggest problems a life could face, and it seems he always found the opportunity behind the problem.

Second, this book does not suggest a naive misunderstanding about the magnitude of life's problems. They are there and they are big. The opportunities will not always outweigh the darkness of the problem, nor are the opportunities always clearly identified in the midst of the problem. But the opportunities are there. It may even be that the size of the problem outweighs the good that can come out of it.

However, our challenge is to personally focus so that our response to the problem becomes more important than the size of the problem. As stated before, the most important thing is what we will make of our circumstances. I don't propose that we blindly ignore the problem, but that we begin to look for the opportunities instead of only dwelling on negative implications of the problem.

The greatest problem is a
missed opportunity.

The tsunami in the Indian Ocean is a good example of this. There is no way that opportunities arising from this natural disaster could ever make up for the loss of life that occurred during the event. However, it was amazing to watch the news stories that showed how communities were brought together, how the world responded to the need, and how God miraculously spared some lives in the midst of the devastation.

While there are opportunities, they do not outweigh the disaster, nor cause us to blindly act as if nothing major happened. The challenge is to look for the good after the bad has already taken place.

When we find ourselves focusing only on the problems, it is easy for the enemy to throw us into a downward spiral in our thought process. This danger leads me to believe that the greatest problem is a missed opportunity.

If we do not proactively seek out the opportunities in life, it is likely that our lives will be a downward spiral of problems. The good news is that many problems are outweighed by the opportunities behind them. With God in control and wanting the best for our lives, He can surely take the problems that Satan intended to destroy us and use them to help us grow in the opportunities behind the problems.

As I once heard a wise preacher say, "We can gaze at our circumstances, and glance at Christ, or we can glance at our circumstances, and gaze at Christ." The choice is ours and our decision will determine whether we are dragged about by the undertow of the circumstances of our life or whether we live in the overflow of God's opportunities in our life.

---

[1] Stephen Covey, Seven *Habits of Highly Effective People* (New York: Simon and Schuster, 1990), p. 65.

47

Opportunities for Discussion

1. Has there ever been an instance in which you were a problem, but you didn't really cause the problem? If so, explain.

   _____

   _____

   _____

2. Do you agree with the statement, "Behind every problem there is an opportunity"?

   Yes_____ No_____

3. Do you tend to be proactive or reactive towards problems that arise in your life?

   _____

4. Do you think you could have weathered the storms that Joseph faced (rejection, slavery)? Where would you have given up?

   _____

   _____

   _____

5. What would keep you from seeing opportunities behind some of your present challenges?

_____

_____

_____

CHAPTER 4

LEARNING TO SEE
OPPORTUNITIES
BEHIND PROBLEMS

There I was six months into the time of transitions in our church. I had accepted every responsibility as a challenge and taken most areas of ministry head on. I was truly running on adrenaline. Our four ministerial staff and two secretaries had been whittled down to me and the two secretaries. And then it happened. I felt like my left arm had been cut off. The secretary who dealt with youth, music, education, and children's ministry announced that she would have to be out for six weeks for major surgery.

And then there were two.

In the days to come the remaining secretary and I would joke about who would be the "last man standing." We tried to laugh to keep from crying. But taking a staff from six to two in a church our size was no laughing matter. We had a real problem.

Or was it an opportunity?

With a lot of help from the Lord and the thoughts of this book beginning to rattle around in my already spinning head, I soon began to see some real opportunities.

The church leadership had already discussed some staffing changes in the future. There was staff salary money just waiting to be used. There were strong lay people available for at least part-time or interim work in the areas where we needed new personnel.

With a little wisdom and vision, the church was able to quickly hire three new part-time staff members who could not only help us get through, but also plant seeds for positions that helped focus our church in the direction we were headed. With a change of perspective, we were able to move from a place where we might barely survive to a place where we really could thrive. That type of thinking is the basis of Opportunity #4: WE HAVE THE OPPORTUNITY TO LET GOD TEACH US TO SEE OPPORTUNITIES BEHIND PROBLEMS.

While this opportunity is similar to opportunity #3 there is a difference. Opportunity #3 establishes the fact that there are opportunities behind problems. Number #4 goes a step farther to indicate that God can actually train our spiritual eyes to look for and identify the opportunities in the midst of the trials of life. There is a difference between simply knowing the opportunities are there, and actually attempting to seek them out in the storm. To know how to actually pursue the opportunities in life, we must undergo a change of perspective.

A Change of Perspective

Seeing things in a new light is not always easy. As a matter of fact it is almost unnatural. Life throws us so many challenges that most people remain beaten down and overwhelmed by their circumstances. It truly takes a trained eye to see the glass as half full, instead of half empty.

To identify how you think and see things look at these four categories of perspective.

Positive or Negative

Most people by nature have either a positive or negative mindset. Some of us would be described as happy-go-lucky. Others seem to have a woe-is-me attitude about life. Some people seem to see the good in everything. Others cannot find anything good even when it is handed to them on a silver platter. Your basic outlook on life greatly affects your ability to see opportunities in the midst of trial. To determine your outlook on life ask yourself the following questions.

- In your conversations and discussions, do you tend to be a positive person or a negative person?
- Is your life more about progress or a downward spiral of negative circumstances?
- When you look over the years of your life, do you find more good to talk about or bad things that have happened to you?
- What comes out of your mouth more—words of complaint or plans for seizing opportunities?
- People who are by nature negative must change the lens they look through in order to see opportunities behind problems.

Thrive or Survive

In our society today it seems that some people thrive in life while others just survive. Those who thrive are always looking for chances to grow and advance. Those who just survive are doing their best just to make it through the day. The thrive or survive mentality shows itself in our bank accounts, our attitudes, our relationships, our family life, our work habits, and just about every area of life. Examine yourself and see if your lifestyle is focused more on surviving or thriving.

- Which of those two words best describes how you handle issues at work, school, and home?
- Do you barely make it by every month financially, mentally and emotionally?

- Can you identify positive growth in any area of your life?
- Are you better or worse off than you were one year, five years, or ten years ago?
- Do you live for the weekend or embrace the day you are in?
- Do you look forward more to going to sleep at night or thinking on the challenges of a new day?

Once again if the answers to these questions reveal a negative slant, you may need to adjust your attitude about life to be able to see the opportunities that may already be present in your life.

Proactive or Reactive

Proactive thinking has already been discussed in the past chapter. Some of us are looking for chances for growth around every corner. For others, life is a series of reactions to circumstances and others actions. Proactive people are constantly looking for a way to advance in every area of life. Reactive people simply get pulled along by whatever life brings their way.

Most people believe that some are just born lucky and that others are born unlucky. The truth is that while some may be more fortunate than others, life is really what you make of it. I have known many rich people who are miserable, and some of the poorest people I have met have the most purpose, peace, and joy. Ask yourself the following questions to determine if you tend to be more proactive or reactive.

- Do you tend to influence your surroundings or do your circumstances influence you?
- Do you spend more time focusing on where you are headed tomorrow or dealing with yesterday's woes?

- At the end of the day, have you accomplished specific goals set at the beginning of the day or have you been dragged along by whatever crisis popped up next?
- Do you have any idea where you are going in life or are you just going where the flow takes you?

A new perspective can change how you deal with the problems that arise in your life and how well you identify opportunities in the midst of life's problems.

Victor or Victim

In today's society you can't go anywhere without seeing someone who plays the victim. In every sector there are those who think that their family, church, employer or government owes them something because of how unfairly they have been treated. God calls us to so much more. Romans 8:37-39 says:

> But in all these things we overwhelmingly conquer through Him who loved us. For I am convinced that neither death, nor life, nor angels, nor principalities, nor things present, nor things to come, nor powers, nor height, nor depth, nor any other created thing, shall be able to separate us from the love of God, which is in Christ Jesus our Lord.

God calls us to be a victor, not a victim. The victim tends to think that the world owes him something, while the victor wants to change the world to make it a better place. The victor looks for a chance to give, while the victim always looks for a chance to get. Through the questions below try to identify whether your tendency is to be a victor or a victim?

- Do you see yourself as being blessed or cursed?
- In your estimation have you given more than you have received?

- Do you usually sense that others owe you or do you see that you have something to offer or contribute for the benefit of others?
- Are you a team player or are you looking out for number one?
- Do you ever do something for someone else without expecting anything in return or is there always a price tag associated with what you have to give?
- Who is more important, you or others? What word best describes you, selfish or selfless?
- Do the answers to these questions call for a fresh look at life?

How you see your importance in relation to others will determine how well you can identify an opportunity behind a problem.

Many times, the greatest change needed is an attitude change.

These four categories of perspective determine how well equipped we are to find the opportunities that life has to offer in both good times and bad. Dealing with these categories shows us that the most crucial change is typically an attitude change. If the questions in this section identify a more negative outlook on life maybe it is time for a change of perspective.

In each of the areas ask the Lord to help you look up instead of down, forward instead of backward. Many times, the greatest change needed is an attitude change.

As God gently changes your viewpoint of life, it will be easier to see the opportunities that He has for you. Joseph seemed to have a handle on his perspective and attitudes as opportunities opened up after just about every trial he faced.

Joseph, the Dreamer in Jail

Joseph surely could have played the victim. Rejected and sold into slavery, he could have blamed his surroundings, but he didn't. In Genesis 39:7-18, life throws Joseph another curve. He was so successful in the service of Potiphar's court that he caught the eye of a very beautiful and important woman, Potiphar's wife.

When we see life through a positive lens, people will want to be around us. We become more attractive and valuable. No one wants to be around a person who feels victimized and whines about his load of dilemmas. Joseph's attractiveness led to his next unexpected opportunity...jail.

That's right, from slavery to the slammer. What a step up. In this passage, Potiphar's wife makes daily inappropriate advances to Joseph. Joseph refuses her offer. Did I mention that morality goes hand in hand with right thinking? Joseph was truly an incredible man. If the average man had suffered Joseph's earlier misfortunes, he would have said, "I deserve this, I've been through so much."

Joseph could have reasoned that no one would ever know. She wanted him and she would never tell. If she did, she would lose her life. But Joseph reasoned rightly. As a matter of fact he reasoned far beyond natural reason. He refused, and refused, and refused. One day when she really pressured him, he refused and ran, leaving his coat behind.

Potiphar's wife could not handle the rejection. How could this Hebrew slave-boy deny her wishes? After all, she was his boss. She screamed and accused Joseph of sexual harassment. And therein Joseph found his next opportunity in jail.

I have had the privilege of doing prison ministry several times. From solitary isolation all the way to a small county jail, I have met prisoners that swear to their innocence and claim that they were victims of someone else's crime. Joseph could have complained and he would have been honest. However, there is no record of this. In jail, there is no record of Joseph complaining or even pressing for early parole. But Scripture does say, "...the chief jailer did not supervise anything under Joseph's charge because the Lord was with Joseph; and whatever he did, the Lord made to prosper" (Genesis 39:23).

Joseph truly made the most of every situation. Every time life dealt him a sorry hand, he made the most of it. He had seen the worst that life has to offer: family rejection, slavery, and prison. But he continued to bloom wherever he was planted. He had learned opportunity #4, the art of seeing God's opportunities behind life's problems.

A Paradigm Shift

It is not certain how Joseph developed these skills, but it is obvious that he thought differently than most. Some would suggest that a loving father is the one who provided Joseph with the framework to see life. Others may say he was just lucky...I don't think so. Many times in these passages, the scripture affirms that the Lord was with Joseph and made him prosper (Genesis 39:2-3; 39:21; 39:23; 42:52; 45:5; 50:20).

As stated before, it is unnatural to see potential when everything looks so negative. To view life this way requires a real paradigm shift. The shift in vision starts as we come before our Creator, and ask Him to change our perspective and give us vision. As He shines His light into our lives, He can help us to see His opportunities behind life's problems.

The next step is to ask God to help us change the outcome of the questions asked earlier to a positive response—to see positive instead of negative, to be proactive instead of reactive, to thrive in life instead of merely surviving, to live as a victor rather than a victim. As we begin to let God change our hearts in these areas, our view of our problems will also change. This process doesn't just change our outlook; it should change our heart, our lifestyle, our responses, and our view of our problems.

A proper perspective of where our problems came from will also help. First, many problems come as a consequence of our bad decisions or actions. Secondly, others come from being related or connected to the people who have made bad decisions. These can be best dealt with through owning up to the poor decision, confessing it, and breaking any habits that may lead to repeated failure.

The second type may require that we end a negative relationship. Or it may mean placing distance in the relationship, so that the negative consequences don't affect us. Then we should own up to our part of the problem, confess it, and move on. These things must be done, because we can't really see the opportunities until we've dealt with the source of the problems.

Still other problems come not in the form of consequences, but just because life can be tough. Sometimes the problems actually make us a part of the problem. Many times there are problems that don't center on us. However, because of our relationship to others, or to the problem itself, we become a part of the problem. In these situations try to implement this series of thoughts:

> I am a problem.
> It's not my problem.
> I'm not going to be a problem.

Sometimes we get caught in situations that are a problem and bring us into the middle of it. The next step is to clarify and make sure that we don't have ownership in the problem.

Did you ask for it? Did you cause it? If not, then it is not your problem, even though you are affected by it. The last step, however, is crucial. We must decide not to respond in a way that makes the problem worse or inflates the issues around the problem. Usually, problems get bigger because of our reaction to them. But we have the choice to end that negative cycle. Remember, Joseph made the most of his negative circumstances; he did not magnify the negative circumstances. Implementing these practical principles into our lives will help us to train ourselves to see His opportunities behind life's problems.

Opportunities for Discussion

1. Which describes you the best? (Circle one word in each pair.)

   a. positive   negative
   b. proactive   reactive
   c. thrive   survive
   d. victor   victim

2. How can you change any negative perspectives you chose above?

   _____

   _____

   Ask God to change your heart and perspective.

3. What have you learned from the life of Joseph?

   _____

   _____

   _____

   _____

   What challenges you the most?

   _____

   _____

4. What is the source of most of your problems?

   _____

   Have you dealt with them? _____ yes _____ no

5. Does your response to your problems make the problem seem bigger or smaller? How will you approach your next problem to make sure that you don't add to it?

   _____

   _____

CHAPTER 5

EXPECTING OPPORTUNITIES AS UNLIKELY CANDIDATES

There I was, standing in the waist-high murky water with all kinds of apprehension running through my mind. Not only were things running through my head, soft gooey clay on the bottom of Lake Tiak-O'Khata was squishing up between my toes. As I looked around me, I easily realized that I was at a great disadvantage. I also realized that compared to my normal setting in a church office, I felt strange and out of place. "What in the world was I thinking? Mangum, what have you gotten yourself into this time?"

A triathlon, that's right. A triathlon is an endurance race event in which individuals compete against each other in three events back-to-back-swimming, biking, and running. In this particular shorter distance event, the course demanded a one-half mile swim, a 27-mile bike ride, and a seven-mile run to cap it off.

Just in case you are picturing a stellar athlete on the other side of this story, let me remind you: I am an overweight associate pastor who is better characterized as chunky than chiseled, more fluffy than fine-tuned. I am not a likely candidate for such an athletic event. As a matter of fact, if you weigh over 200 lbs in these events, you can race under the classification "Clydesdale". That is what I was going for, the fastest of the fat men. Nevertheless, I was determined to complete the course.

So there I stood, in line to start my swim. Surrounded by what in my mind looked like Olympiads, ultra men and women, and stallions. I wondered if I could sneak away unnoticed. Somehow God gave me the courage to finish what I had started. While I didn't even come close to any prize money, I finished a few minutes faster than my goal and was pleased with my experience.

I was an unlikely candidate to participate in such an athletic event. Most people see themselves as unlikely candidates to receive all that God has for them. All of this just proves Opportunity #5: WE HAVE THE OPPORTUNITY TO RECEIVE OPPORTUNITIES AS UNLIKELY PEOPLE. In a way, I had no business participating in the triathlon. However, I was determined. If we have determination and commitment in Christ, He can help the most unlikely people do the most extraordinary things.

The Leadership Cycle

People come and people go. Leaders are not an exception to the rule. No matter how strong a human leader is, there will be a day when his leadership influence will be remembered and learned from, but he will be gone from the scene. Death, geographical moves, and change of vision and direction leave vacancies in leadership positions every day. There is, therefore, none who is indispensable in his role.

I was recently visiting a 98-year-old man in the hospital. The man had been a very successful doctor in our community for years. He was wealthy, successful, and powerful in his prime. But as a 98-year-old, he was frail and fragile, and to many who had highly esteemed him in his prime, he was forgotten. I remember thinking how ironic it was that a man who had brought healing to so many now was at the mercy of other men and ultimately God to lengthen his life. Not long after the visit, the gentleman passed away. No matter who we are, we are all dispensable.

With such a leadership cycle, God provides common, ordinary people with the chance to rise up and seize opportunities. No matter who you are, you have the chance to step up, be counted, and make a difference in your world.

> *In life there are spectators*
> *and there are participants.*
> *Which one will you be?*

God has a plan for you. Jeremiah 29:11 reminds us, "'For I know the plans that I have for you' declares the LORD, 'plans for welfare and not for calamity to give you a future and a hope.'"

And even behind our toughest challenges there are opportunities. Someone well said, "In life there are spectators and there are participants." You have a choice to make. You will either make the choice to sit on the sidelines of life and watch the opportunities pass you by, or you will get up off the bench and get in the game.

Joseph from Prison to Prime Minister

In Chapter 4, we last left Joseph in a dark musty Egyptian prison cell. Opportunity #5 definitely applies to Joseph. In this case, Joseph was a weak and unlikely candidate to expect God's opportunities. God gave Joseph opportunities as a weak and unlikely person. But beyond that, Joseph wasn't just unlikely; he had all the cards stacked against him. Rejected by family, sold into slavery, thrown into jail, Joseph was beyond unlikely.

To top it off, he was a Hebrew in Egypt. Egypt was not exactly the land of opportunities for Hebrews. Egyptians hated Hebrews. They made them slaves and wouldn't even sit at the same table with them to eat. Genesis 43:32 says, "So they served him by himself, and them by themselves, and the Egyptians who ate with him by themselves, because the Egyptians could not eat bread with the Hebrews, for that was loathsome to the Egyptians." It was unthinkable for an Egyptian to entertain the company of a Hebrew. To say that Joseph was an unlikely candidate for opportunity in this situation is a huge understatement.

But God gave him the opportunity anyway.

God seems to take delight in using ordinary people to do extraordinary things. In Genesis 40 and 41, Joseph became known for his ability to interpret dreams. In Chapter 40, he accurately interpreted the dreams of two of Pharaoh's officials, the chief cupbearer and the baker.

The result of the cupbearer's dream is that he was freed from prison and restored to his position of power. Joseph asked the cupbearer to remember him and put in a good word to get him out of jail, but the ungrateful cupbearer forgot Joseph.

Was this a mistake, a missed opportunity, an injustice to Joseph? In the big picture it is absolutely not. It was just God's timing for Joseph's opportunity. Two full years later, Pharaoh had two disturbing dreams that he needed interpreted. That was when God prompted the cupbearer to remember Joseph. The cupbearer related to Pharaoh Joseph's ability to interpret dreams. So Pharaoh called for Joseph from prison to interpret his dreams.

The dreams that Joseph interpreted for Pharaoh predicted that Egypt would have seven years of plenty and abundance. These seven years would be followed by seven years of drought and famine. Then Joseph moved from interpreting dreams to giving advice. He told Pharaoh that he should look for a discerning and wise man to put in charge of Egypt. The man should take one-fifth of the produce during the years of abundance and store it for the years of famine.

Just imagine the picture. The loathsome Hebrew who is fresh out of prison is standing before possibly the most powerful man in the known world at that time telling him how he should order his affairs. Not only does he interpret the dream, he has the gall to predict disaster for the strongest nation in the world.

Beyond that, he seems at ease telling Pharaoh not only what he should do, but also how to do it. Joseph does everything but drop his own name for the position of power that he had suggested. The scene is almost unbelievable unless you look at it through the lens of opportunity. When God is in control, He makes opportunities for the most unlikely people in the most unlikely circumstances.

What happens next just puts the exclamation point on the principles of this book. Pharaoh looks at Joseph and says,

> "Since God has informed you of all this, there is no one so discerning and wise as you are. You shall be over my house, and according to your command all my people shall do homage; only in the throne I will be greater than you. See I have set you over all the land of Egypt" (Genesis 41:39-41).

He went from prisoner in the morning to prince in the afternoon. From rags to riches. Now he stood with the king's signet ring of authority on his hand, fine clothes on his back, and a gold necklace around his neck.

Only God could have conceived such a plan to use Joseph for such an opportunity.

God's Plans are Bigger than Ours

Joseph's story illustrates the fact that God's plans are bigger than our own. Joseph was known from way back to be a big dreamer, but even in his wildest childhood dreams he could never have dreamed that he would be placed in power over the most powerful country in the world. God's plan did not unfold as Joseph would have planned it. But it unfolded perfectly.

If Joseph had written the story himself, he probably would have skipped the slavery, the accusations of impropriety, and the imprisonment. But we must keep in mind that God is the author and hero of all of our stories and not the other way around. The interesting twists and turns in the plot of our lives and Joseph's bring us to an understanding of these following truths:

- God's plan is not always our plan.
- God's plan is bigger than our plan.
- God's timing is not our timing.
- God can make the relationships and circumstances surrounding our lives intersect and connect at the right time to fulfill his plan.
- The trouble that we face along life's way may be part of the plot to bring us to the realization of God's opportunities.

God's Word in Isaiah backs these truths:

"For my thoughts are not your thoughts, nor are your ways my ways," declares the Lord. "For as high as the heavens are higher than the earth, so are my ways higher than your ways, and my thoughts than your thoughts" (Isaiah 55:8-9).

It is in the creativity and thoroughness of God's plan that we can be assured that He can do extraordinary things with ordinary people. You may feel that you have nothing to offer and that you are an unlikely candidate to do great things for God but take it from Joseph and me, life has better things in store for you. It is time that you open your eyes and see what God would do through your life and even through your troubles.

Opportunities for Discussion

1. Who are some influential people that you would see as indispensable in your life?

   _____

2. What leadership vacuums might God want you to fill in your home, church, or work?

   _____

3. Do you see yourself as a likely or unlikely person for God to use to do extraordinary things? Why?

   _____

   _____

4. Joseph had the gift of interpreting dreams. What gifts has God given you that He may want you to use in the unfolding of His plan?

   _____

   _____

5. Which of the five principles about God's plans is easiest for you to accept? Which is hardest for you to accept? Why?

   1. God's plan is not always our plan.
   2. God's plan is bigger than our plan.
   3. God's timing is not our timing.

4. God can make the relationships and circumstances surrounding our lives intersect and connect at the right time to fulfill his plan.

5. The trouble that we face along life's way may be part of the plot to bring us to the realization of God's opportunities

   Easiest _____

   Hardest _____

6. Do you feel that God's dreams for you are bigger than your dreams for yourself? Why or why not?

   _____

   _____

CHAPTER SIX

PREPARING FOR FUTURE OPPORTUNITIES

There I was standing in the middle of a real mess. The smell of smoke pierced my nostrils. The dark smoke-stained walls left an eerie uncomfortable feeling. The smoke stains covered the colors that had once been there. Cool dampness brought feelings of anything but comfort and home. Sheetrock sagged and charred blown insulation lay scattered on the ground.

The charred cabinets barely clung to the walls. The kitchen looked more like a war zone than a place to cook a Thanksgiving feast. Damage from a fireman's high-pressure hose was evident throughout the house.

And then I heard the strangest thing come out of my mouth... "I'll take it, I'll be glad to buy your house."

What was I thinking? Who would want the hassle of this burned out house? The kitchen and living area were destroyed by fire and smoke. Every other room in the house had been permeated by smoke and soot. But I said it! "I'll be glad to take it, and I'll pay my hard earned money for the joy of taking on this mess."

In the midst of being a husband, the father of four young children, and a full time youth pastor facing the needs of some eighty teenagers, when was I going to be able to do anything with this house?

Seven months later some of these questions were answered. After gutting much of the house and painting the rest of it, the opportunities began to shine through. God had blessed us with the opportunity of having about 1000 more square feet of living space and an extra bedroom, bathroom, and game room for our growing family for about the same price as the house we were living in. Sure, it was a lot of work, but seeing God's opportunities means being able to look past the soot and smoke of life. God's opportunities become a lot clearer with a little vision and a lot of determination.

God Gives Us What We Need

It would be a huge understatement to say that all we need to grasp God's opportunities is vision and determination. The other missing piece of the equation is preparation. It is God preparing us that equips us for all of the opportunities He has for us. His preparation is the key to Opportunity #6: WE HAVE THE OPPORTUNITY TO BE PREPARED FOR OUR FUTURE. God prepares us for the future through experiences, trials, gifts and callings.

God prepares us for the future through experiences, trials, gifts and callings.

Experiences

I was not intimidated by the huge task of remodeling a burned out house because I had experience working with a builder in college. That experience gave me the ability to see an unfinished project as finished. The experience prepared me for the opportunity.

God always prepares us for the opportunities that He has in store for us. The principle is found throughout Scripture, "He who is faithful in a small thing will be given much" (Luke 16:10, Matthew 25:21). Throughout the course of our life, He gives us small accomplishments and experiences that prepare us for the opportunities that He wants to give us later.

God used the experiences that I had in college, seminary, and other church positions to prepare me for the opportunity to serve in a church where I was left as the only pastoral staff. Whether we see it or not, God is training us daily for things He has for us in the future.

Trials

Every small trial or test we go through in life prepares us for other things we will face down the road in life. The most difficult things in life can be used to prepare us by toughening, strengthening, and teaching us to trust God's hand completely. Many times we go through trials that will be used as an opportunity to help others through similar trials later in life. Consider the words of the Apostle Paul: "The God of all comfort comforts us in all afflictions so that we will be able to comfort those who are in any affliction with the comfort with which we ourselves are comforted by God" (2 Corinthians 1:4).

God uses the trials in our lives so He can use us as tools to help others through similar trials. For example one of the biggest trials of my life was my parents' divorce. But God has used that event to instill in me a strong desire for a solid marriage myself, as well as to prepare me to help many teenagers through the difficult trial of their parents' divorce. God even prepares us in our pain. But He promises that He will never give us more than we can bear (1 Corinthians 10:13).

Gifts

God's Word teaches that God gives us gifts in our lives that are for the good of other people (Romans 12, Ephesians 4, and 1 Corinthians 12-14). The gifts and talents He has given us match us with the opportunities He will send us. Billy Graham is a good example of this. Dr. Graham has had the opportunity to be instrumental in leading millions of people to Christ all over the world. His messages are not complicated and his delivery is straightforward but not extraordinary.

Who would question that Billy Graham's effectiveness as an evangelist has come from a special giftedness from the Lord? God prepared him with a great gift for a great opportunity. I once did construction work for one of Dr. Graham's relatives. She said that at family gatherings, he tends to be quiet and reserved. Being a great evangelist is his gift, not his innate personality.

Callings

Romans 11:29 says that "the gifts and the callings of God are irrevocable." God uses gifts and His call in our lives hand in hand to prepare us for His opportunities. The writer of those words would know it best. The Apostle Paul was called to be the messenger to the non-Jewish world. Acts 16:9 records a specific call to an opportunity for Paul to speak to the Macedonians.

Paul's past, his training, his trials, his experiences, his gifts, and now this calling were all combined to give him the opportunity to be the apostle who would spread the gospel all over the Mediterranean world and become the author of 13 New Testament books. Paul is a great example of how God prepares us for opportunities.

Preparing a Prince

Joseph's journey to becoming the most powerful person in all of Egypt is likewise an illustration of how God prepares a person for opportunity. Think about the things that were a part of Joseph's life, one piece building on another, to help prepare him for his opportunity. As a boy, Joseph dreamed and understood dreams. This was not only an experience in his life but also a gift from God.

When Joseph was in jail years later, God used this experience and gift again with the cupbearer and baker and finally this gift and experience gave Joseph an audience with Pharaoh. This series of events launched him into the greatest opportunity in his life. What about Joseph's trials? God prepared Joseph in the pit for the trials of slavery. The bondage of slavery was then used to prepare him for the bondage of prison. All the while, these trials were being used to teach Joseph to be patient for the fulfillment of his childhood dreams.

Those early dreams of ruling over his brothers would not come true until Joseph was thirty years old. (Genesis 41:46) Joseph had stored the grain during the seven years of plenty and then the famine came. Genesis 41:57 records that people from all over the earth came to Egypt for aid during the famine. That large group of people included Joseph's brothers. They left the land of Canaan to go to Egypt to get grain.

Upon their arrival in Egypt, Joseph recognized his brothers, but they did not recognize him. Immediately, upon seeing them Joseph remembered the childhood dreams that he had about them (42:9). Joseph did not want to dominate or rule over them. But thirteen years before, God had called Joseph not only to rule them, but also to save them and the rest of the world from famine.

Joseph's opportunity had more to do with God's salvation than it did Joseph's personal promotion. Upon seeing his brothers, Joseph was faced with the biggest challenge of his life. Would he respond in revenge or in kindness?

Once again God had prepared Joseph for even this challenge. God had spared Joseph's life in the pit. God gave Joseph favor in Potiphar's eyes. God spared Joseph's life again when Potiphar's wife accused him of assaulting her. God showed favor and prospered Joseph even in prison.

Throughout Joseph's life God had demonstrated kindness, favor, mercy, and grace. How would Joseph respond? Would he respond to his natural feelings of revenge and anger or would he respond in the way God had prepared him through his own divine example of kindness?

In Genesis 45:1-5 Joseph was overwhelmed with the emotion and responsibility of this decision. He could not control himself any longer. He sent everyone else away so that he could reveal himself to his brothers. He said,

> "Please, come closer to me ....I am your brother Joseph, whom you sold into Egypt. Now do not be grieved or angry with yourselves, because you sold me here, for God sent me before you to preserve life....God sent me before you to preserve for you a remnant in the earth, and to keep you alive by a great deliverance. Now, therefore, it was not you who sent me here, but God"(Genesis 45:4-8).

Joseph chose kindness. He had an understanding that his experiences, gifts, callings, and even his trials were used by God to prepare him for this opportunity. When Pharaoh heard of this strange turn of events, he told Joseph to send for his family, and bring them to Egypt, and he would give them the best of the land. Joseph's entire family moved to the land of Egypt to be saved from the remaining five years of famine. So God had prepared and used Joseph to save the world from famine and death and to bring his family to prosperity.

Our Greatest Opportunity

In this portion of Joseph's life, we catch a glimpse of our greatest opportunity — to share the kindness of God. God truly had prepared Joseph for many opportunities, but the greatest opportunity was for Joseph to show the same type of kindness and grace that God had shown him. No matter what opportunities this book may cause us to search for and to identify, the greatest opportunity will be to share the grace of God with our fellow man.

All of our life's experiences, trials, gifts and callings are aimed at helping us seize various opportunities, but the greatest is to share the grace of God that He has already given us. Will you respond as a person of grace in a tumultuous world of hurt and pain?

As you contemplate that question, understand that in the process, God may break through some of the binding laws of man. He did with Joseph. A Hebrew ruling Egypt? A prisoner becoming a Prince? Slaves being used to save? Dreams that come true?

In all these ways God showed that man's preconceived ideas and laws can be overturned by a God of extreme opportunities.

Are you bound by the views and laws of man? God's opportunities could break you out of the pit of poverty, the slavery of a dead-end job, the prison of depression and fear. I can guarantee that if we will let God use our experiences, trials, gifts and callings for His opportunities, He can use us to do extraordinary things beyond our wildest dreams.

Remember, "He is able to do far more abundantly beyond all that we ask or think" (Ephesians 3:20). Let Him prepare you for great things!

Opportunities for Discussion

1. Do you find it easy to find potential in people or projects similar to the burned out house? (List some.)

   _____

   _____

   _____

2. What experiences, trials, gifts and callings are in your life that God could be using to prepare you for great opportunities?

   _____

   _____

   _____

3. What opportunities does God seem to be preparing you for in light of question #2?

   _____

   _____

4. Do you agree that Joseph's greatest opportunity was to share God's grace? Why or why not?

   _____

   _____

5. What opportunities to share God's grace are you prepared for?

_____

_____

_____

6. What laws of man could God break in helping you seize your opportunities?

_____

_____

_____

CHAPTER 7

CHOOSING BETWEEN
OUR PLANS
AND HIS OPPORTUNITIES

There you are, wondering if anything in this book applies to you. Most people who read this book will be living in a place where they hope things will get better. Most of us go through life just getting by. There is no sense of adventure. There is no sense of living for something bigger than ourselves and our circumstances. Most of us have just gotten comfortable with status quo. If you are one of those, I hope that you are challenged to look beyond the circumstances and beyond the monotony of life to see some new opportunities for yourself.

There are a rare few readers who already live at the pinnacle of life's experience, claiming God's blessing, and seizing opportunities. For you I hope that you are challenged to look for the next peak of opportunity beyond the ridge you are already on. Most of all, my prayer would be that every reader would minimize the problems that they face in life and maximize the potential of opportunities in the future.

The six opportunities presented in this book so far are:

- Recognize that God as in control.
- Allow any circumstances to strengthen us.
- Identify an opportunity behind every problem.
- Let God train us to see problems as opportunities.
- Be effective as weak and unlikely people.
- Be prepared for our future.

These six opportunities lead us to the last and most important of all the opportunities. Opportunity #7: WE HAVE THE OPPORTUNITY TO CHOOSE OUR PLANS OR HIS PLANS FOR OUR LIFES.

When I look back over my life and some of the stories I have included on these pages, I don't see my plan. I see God's plan. If I had the opportunity to be the author of my life from the beginning, I would not have included my parents' divorce, the difficult staffing situation at my church, or the purchase of a burnt-out house.

If we could write our own life stories, would we have included the trials and tough times? Yet, as we look back on the difficult times in our lives, it is those times that strengthen us the most. Now as I look back on my life, I would not trade how God used those events to strengthen me. Each trial we face has the potential of making us into a greater person.

We all could resist God's plans for our lives. But opportunity #7 shows us that we have the choice to go our own way or to choose God's plans for our lives—trials and all. Accepting God's plans for our lives allows us to say, "While I don't know what the future holds, I do know *who* holds the future."

The heartbeat of opportunity #7 is found in Proverbs 3:5-6: "Trust in the Lord with all your heart and do not lean on your own understanding. In all your ways acknowledge Him and He will make your paths straight." Practicing this opportunity requires a great deal of trust. It also takes a willingness to yield our rights to God's control. This is what it means to not lean on our own understanding.

This opportunity outweighs all the others because it requires us to apply all of the others. This opportunity calls us to yield to God's control and His plan. It forces us out of the role of the reactive survivor, victim, and pessimist into the role of a thriving, proactive victor and optimist.

The truth is some people do not want to make that transition. Some people have become addicted to their negative circumstances. They use life's problems as their crutch and excuse for all of their failures. Opportunity #7 causes you to put the crutch down and trust God. It means literally giving thanks in all things (I Thessalonians 5:18) and even receiving trials as a part of God's plan for opportunities.

Will you live in the overflow,
or be dragged down
by the undertow?

Frankly, it is a choice. Better yet it may be **the choice**. It becomes the person's choice to live in the overflow of God's goodness instead of being dragged along by the undertow of life's circumstances. How can we say that we have accepted Christ as Savior and Lord, and willingly live in more obedience to the trials that we have encountered by complaining about our life?

Whether or not we choose to see things from His perspective and accept His plan has far reaching consequences. It determines the legacy that we leave behind.

Joseph's Legacy

Joseph definitely understood opportunity #7. He gladly accepted God's plan for his life. What if he had been the author of his own story? Like many of us, he would surely have left out jealous brothers, the pit, Potiphar's wife, prison, and famine. However, it was all these things that strengthened him, that made him a man of God.

What if he had decided to take matters into his own hands instead of trusting in God's plan? Think of how the story would have changed if Joseph had just acted on human instinct. He could have fought with his brothers at the site of the pit and been killed by them. He could have had an affair with Potiphar's wife. He could have decided that he was tired of dreaming in prison and not interpreted the baker's and cupbearer's dreams. He could have avoided future political negotiations with Pharaoh based on his poor political past with Potiphar. He could have focused more on making himself the most wealthy, most powerful man in the world instead of saving the world from famine.

But he didn't. At each one of these turns in the path of Joseph's life, he accepted his circumstances, trusted in God's plan, and rose above typical human instinct. He was willing to accept God's plan for His life, instead of his own plans. He understood Jeremiah's words long before they were written: "For I know the plans that I have for you," declares the Lord, "plans for welfare and not for calamity to give you a future and a hope" (Jeremiah 29:11).

No one would question that Joseph applied opportunity #7. He clearly accepted and fulfilled God's plan for his life. He made the most out of the good and the bad things that were thrown his way. He would gladly agree with the words of the Apostle Paul:

Not that I speak from want, for I have learned to be content in whatever circumstances I am. I know how to get along with humble means, and also how to live in prosperity; in any and every circumstance, I have learned the secret of being filled and going hungry, both of having abundance and suffering need. *I can*

do all things through Christ who strengthens me
(Philippians 4:11-13, emphasis added).

Joseph knew how to make the most of the best and the
worst of life. I know many people who would have climbed
out of Joseph's pit, checked into a psychiatric ward due to
emotional instability, and missed out on the rest of God's
opportunities. It takes perseverance and faith to apply opportunity #7. Joseph had that perseverance and faith. He made
the choice to accept God's plan for his life.

Joseph demonstrates his perseverance and faith even on
the occasion of his father's death. When Joseph's brothers
saw that their father was dead, they said, "What if Joseph
bears a grudge against us and pays us back in full for all
the wrong which we did to him?" (Genesis 50:15). They did
not understand that an opportunity lifestyle does not hold
grudges.

They went on to contrive a plan. They sent to Joseph a
messenger who said, "Your father charged us before he died
saying, 'Thus you shall say to Joseph, "Please forgive I beg
you, the transgressions of your brothers and their sin, for
they did you wrong."'" I guess they felt like a little lie would
help the matter. Jacob had sent no such message.

Nevertheless, Joseph responded in grace. He wept and
said:

Do not be afraid, for am I in God's place? As for you,
you meant evil against me, but God meant it for good
in order to bring about this present result, to preserve
many people's lives. So therefore, do not be afraid;
I will provide for you and your little ones (Genesis
50:19-21).

Joseph was able to speak kindly to his brothers because
he had accepted God's plan for his life. It was easy to not

hold a grudge because God's plan does not make room for a grudge. Grudges weigh down; they don't help us see the opportunities God has for us. Joseph could forgive, only because he was settled with God's overall plan for his life.

A Change of Outlook

Joseph chose to have a different outlook on life than most people because he chose to apply opportunity #7. Will you accept that challenge? Are you resolved to receive God's plan for your life?

I have heard it said of some people that everything they touch turns to gold. With the thoughts of this book in mind, I would like to add an extra thought to that saying. I believe that, to some extent, there *are* those for whom everything they touch turns to gold. Unfortunately, others just don't reach out to touch anything or anyone. If you don't see any opportunities in your life, it may be that you haven't looked for them or reached out for them.

Keep in mind, there is a sovereign God who has a plan for your life. He is a good and benevolent God, so the plan must be the best for you, if it reflects His character. His plan is there for you to accept.

The start of this plan is for you to accept the plan of forgiveness through the death of His son, Jesus Christ. John 1:12 says, "As many as received Him for them He gave the right to become children of God, even those who would believe on His name." I encourage you to receive not only God's plan of salvation, but His entire plan for your life. He has the plan and has even paid the price for the fulfillment of the plan. But He gives you the choice whether or not to accept it! I promise you will never lack adventure and opportunity.

Opportunities for Discussion

1. Do you see yourself as just getting by or thriving in your life?

_____

_____

2. Will you stop and pray that God will show you opportunities that He has for you?

3. Of the seven opportunities that have been presented, which is the hardest for you to accept? Why?

   1. We have the opportunity to recognize that God is in control.
   2. We have the opportunity to allow any circumstance to strengthen us.
   3. We have the opportunity to identify an opportunity behind every problem.
   4. We have the opportunity to let God train us to see problems as opportunities.
   5. We have the opportunity to be effective as weak and unlikely people.
   6. We have the opportunity to be prepared for our future.
   7. We have the opportunity to choose our plans or His opportunities.

4. Could you have been as forgiving as Joseph was to his brothers?

5. Have you ever accepted God's plan for your forgiveness through His son, Jesus Christ? If not, why not pray the following prayer to receive it now?

   "Dear God, I know that I have often walked away from your plan. I thank you for the forgiveness you provided through your son Jesus on the cross. Forgive me of any wrongs and help me see the opportunities you have for my life. Thank you for making me your child."

6. Are you willing to seize the opportunity to accept God's overall plan for your life? What do you think it holds?

   _____

   _____

7. What part of His plan is:

   A. easiest for you to accept?

   B. hardest for you to accept?

CHAPTER 8

PASSING ON A LIFESTYLE OF OPPORTUNITY

There I was sitting at our kitchen counter thinking I was about to finish my first book and then God showed me one more very important opportunity. Opportunity #8: WE HAVE THE OPPORTUNITY TO PASS ON A LIFESTYLE OF OPPORTUNITY. So many people live below or at a level of mediocrity. The message of God's wonderful opportunities needs to be passed on.

If anything in this book has moved you to look at life through a different lens or seize an opportunity, then pass it on. The ideas found in the pages of this book did not come to me naturally. As a matter of fact, I am by nature quite cynical. Without Christ in my life, I would be down-right negative and pessimistic.

God has changed my outlook on life. He used others to pass an attitude of hope in my direction. I can't claim ownership of one thought in this book. They were all passed to me by someone else. I am obligated to pass them on to others. I hope that you will see passing this lifestyle on as your greatest opportunity.

Joseph passed it on

Joseph not only received God's plan for his life, he went beyond that. He passed on a lifestyle of opportunity and hope. The last words of Joseph's life show that he not only had an understanding of a lifestyle of opportunity, but a willingness to pass it on.

In Genesis 50:24 Joseph calls his brothers and sons to himself and says,

> "I am about to die, but God will surely take care of you and bring you up from this land, to the land which He promised on oath to Abraham, to Isaac, and to Jacob...God will surely take care of you, and you shall carry my bones up from here."

Even in his closing breath, Joseph showed he was a man of hope and opportunity. For starters, he stares death in the face, but has his eyes set on the bigger picture. At the point of death, he wasn't thinking of himself—but of the next generation and their ability to realize the dream and opportunity promised to Abraham generations earlier.

He let them know that God is in control and will bring the dream to fruition. He promised that God will take care of them and be true to His word. God would give them great opportunities. Joseph was passing the baton of hope and opportunity to the next generation. He knew he had the opportunity to pass on the lifestyle that he himself had exemplified.

Pass it On

You too can seize opportunity #8 and pass on a lifestyle of hope. 2 Timothy 2:2 says, "These things which you have heard from me in the presence of many witnesses, entrust these to faithful men who will be able to teach others also."

*Passing on a lifestyle of hope
is your greatest opportunity.*

You can pass on a lifestyle of hope. Passing on a lifestyle of hope is your greatest opportunity. You can do that by simply telling others what you have read. You can even choose some friends or family who are stuck in a lifestyle of defeat and get them a copy of this book.

But I would suggest something even bigger. *Live it!* Live it and pass it on.

Your actions will speak louder than your words. Wouldn't you love to be remembered as a person who seized all the opportunities God gave you? You can be remembered that way.

If you apply the opportunities cited in this book, there is no telling what God might do with your life. So, watch carefully, live loudly, and listen closely because *opportunity knocks.*

Printed in the United States
64621LVS00002B/313-501

9 781600 346170